# Science Experiments with Simple Machines
## Simple Experiments with
# Screws

Chris Oxlade

WINDMILL
BOOKS
New York

Published in 2014 by Windmill Books, An Imprint of Rosen Publishing
29 East 21st Street, New York, NY 10010

Produced for Windmill by Calcium Creative Ltd
Editors for Calcium Creative Ltd: Sarah Eason and Jennifer Sanderson
Designer: Emma DeBanks

Photo Credits: Cover: Shutterstock: Stephen Mcsweeny. Inside: Dreamstime:
Monika Adamczyk 9, Dmitry Kalinovsky 14, Kone 28, Iurii Konoval 25, Nicolescu
21, Luis Santos 4, Razvan Shutterwolf 16, Steveheap 7, Stratum 8, Igor
Vesninoff 17, Joachim Wendler 13; Shutterstock: AKV 1, 29, Gualtiero Boffi
15, James Clarke 6, Morphart Creation 20, Zdenek Rosenthaler 5, Shkonst 23,
Tish1 12, Toshi12 24, Yulia 22; Tudor Photography 10, 11, 18, 19, 26, 27.

Library of Congress Cataloging-in-Publication Data

Oxlade, Chris.
Simple experiments with screws / by Chris Oxlade.
pages cm. — (Science experiments with simple machines)
Includes index.
ISBN 978-1-61533-753-8 (library binding) — ISBN 978-1-61533-823-8 (pbk.) —
ISBN 978-1-61533-824-5 (6-pack)
1. Screws—Experiments—Juvenile literature. 2. Screw–threads—
Experiments—Juvenile literature. 3. Bolts and nuts—Experiments—Juvenile
literature. I. Title.
TJ1338.O894 2014
621.8'82078—dc23
2013003808

Manufactured in the United States of America

CPSIA Compliance Information: Batch #BS13WM: For Further Information contact Windmill Books, New York, New York at 1-866-478-0556

# Contents

# Simple Machines

What do you think of when you hear the word "machine?" Perhaps you imagine a car, a robot, or even a lawn mower. Machines are things that make our lives easier, by helping us do jobs. Cars, robots, and lawn mowers are complicated machines made up of thousands of parts. However, many machines are very simple. They have only one or two parts. **Screws** are one type of simple machine.

## Types of Simple Machines

There are six types of simple machines. Screws are one. The others are **wheel and axles**, **pulleys**, **levers**, **wedges**, and **inclined planes**. Some of these machines do not really look like machines. Some do not have any moving parts. However, they still help us do jobs in our everyday lives.

*A corkscrew uses a screw to pull corks from bottles.*

*Nuts, bolts, and screws all have screw threads.*

## What Is a screw?

Screws are used to connect things together. One example is the small screw that fixes the cover on a toy's battery box. The simple machine called a screw is the spiral thread around one of these screws. This is also called a **screw thread**. In this book, you will find many examples of screws in action. There are also some interesting experiments for you to do. Try them out and discover for yourself how screws work.

# How Screw Threads Work

A screw thread is a spiral thread made up of a groove and a ridge. Screw threads are found on bolts and screws, and on some other parts of machines. When you turn a bolt or a screw, the groove pulls or pushes against something, which could be a nut or a material, such as wood.

## Screw Parts

Most screws and bolts are made of steel, which is very strong, because the **forces** on them can be very large. Some screws are also made from aluminium and brass. Bolts can also be made from tough plastics, such as nylon, and a few are made from hard types of wood. Most screw threads are right-handed. This means that when you turn a screw thread clockwise, the thread will make it move away from you.

Thread

You can see the sharp edge and groove that make the screw thread on this screw.

Turning a screw clockwise makes it move into wood.

## Pushes and Pulls

In this book you will see the words "force," "effort," and "**load**." A force is a push or a pull. Simple machines change the direction or **magnitude** of forces. An effort is a force that you make on a simple machine. The load is the **weight** or other force that a machine moves.

# Fixing Things with Screws

Screw threads are good for fixing materials together, and for fixing objects to materials, such as wood, metal, plastic, and stonework. The screw thread pulls tightly into a material, or into the screw thread in another piece of material.

## Wood Screws and Fixing Screws

Wood screws are designed for fixing pieces of wood together, or for attaching objects, such as metal hinges or plastic handles, onto wood. They are called screws because they have a screw thread along them. Fixing screws are similar, but designed to attach things to brick or stone.

*This wood screw will hold the hinge tightly against the wood.*

## The Parts of a Screw

A screw is made up of a shaft with its screw thread. It has a head at one end and a sharp point at the other end. The head is wider than the shaft and has a slot in it for the tip of a screwdriver to fit into. The pointed end works as a wedge. It pushes material apart as the screw is screwed in.

## Screw Caps

There are threads on the inside of a screw cap and the neck of the bottle, which fit together. When you turn the cap, the thread pulls it down onto the bottle, making an airtight seal. Food and storage jars work in the same way.

When the lid is on, the thread on this honey jar makes sure that the jar is properly sealed.

# The Force of Screws

You can feel the force made by a screw by trying this simple experiment with a metal screw. A screw burrows into wood when you turn it.

**You Will Need:**

- A large screw
- A small screw
- A screwdriver to fit your screws
- A bradawl
- A waste piece of softwood
- An adult

**1** Hold the thread of the large screw between your fingers on one hand. Use the fingers of your other hand to turn the head of the screw clockwise. Feel how the screw thread pulls on your fingers. Turn the screw counterclockwise to make the screw push instead of pull.

**2** Use a **bradawl** to make a small hole in the piece of softwood. Try pushing a small screw into the hole with your hand. Now try turning the screw with a screwdriver (ask an adult to hold the wood for you if you need help). Compare the effort you made with your fingers with the effort you with a screwdriver.

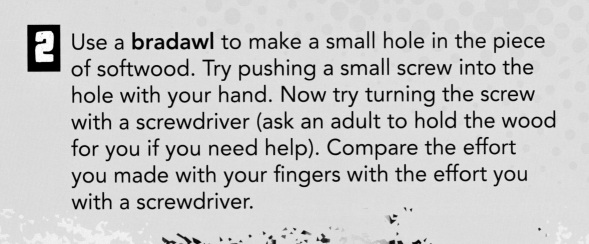

So Simple!

With the screw in your fingers, you could feel the pull that the thread made as you turned the screw. The screw changed a small turning force into a strong pulling force (or a strong pushing force). It is impossible to push a screw into wood. Yet, when you used a screwdriver, the thread pulled strongly on the wood, and this pushed the screw into the wood.

11

# Nuts and Bolts

Nuts and bolts are another way of joining materials together and of fixing things in place. A bolt is a rod of material with thread around it. It is the same width all the way along its length and has no sharp point.

## Doing Up Nuts and Bolts

A nut fits onto a bolt. It has a hole in the center, with a thread around the inside of the hole. It will fit only on a bolt of the same size. The head of a bolt is a square or a **hexagonal** shape, so that a wrench can fit onto it. Nuts are the same shape. Turning the nut and bolt in opposite directions makes the nut move along the bolt.

*You can see the interlocking screw threads on these nuts and bolts.*

Bolt

Nut

# Tightening Bolts

Imagine fixing two pieces of metal together, such as the parts of bed frame. Each piece has a hole that the shaft of a bolt fits through. To fix them together with a nut and bolt, you would line up the holes, push the bolt through, and put a nut on the end. Then you would turn the nut and bolt with a wrench. A screw thread increases the effort you make, so the pieces of metal are squeezed tightly together.

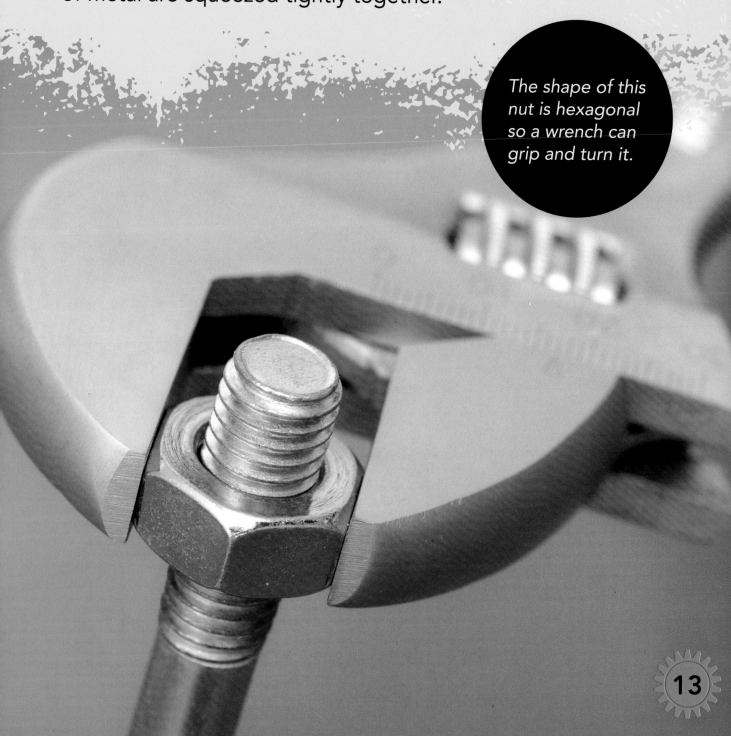

*The shape of this nut is hexagonal so a wrench can grip and turn it.*

# Nuts and Bolts at Work

Nut and bolts hold together the parts of many different objects and machines, from chairs to aircraft. Some big machines contain thousands and thousands of nuts and bolts. Without nuts and bolts, they would fall apart!

## Bolts in Building

Many buildings are held up by a strong steel frame. The frame is made in several sections. On the building site, the sections are fixed tightly together with large, super-strong nuts and bolts. Construction workers tighten the nuts and bolts with huge wrenches.

*This construction worker is joining two steel sections of a building with nuts and bolts.*

## Wheel Bolts

Vehicle wheels are attached to wheel hubs by strong bolts. There are at least four bolts on each wheel of a car, and many more on truck wheels. The bolts pass through the wheel and screw into holes in the hub. The nuts must be done up very tightly to stop the wheel from falling off as it spins at high speed.

*Plumbers use wrenches to tighten joints on a water pipe.*

## Pipe Joints

Some types of pipe joint are held together by screw threads. The end of a piece of pipe fits snugly into the joint. Then a metal hoop and a nut are put over the pipe. The nut fits onto a thread on the joint. When it is tightened, the nut squashes the hoop onto the pipe to make a strong, watertight joint.

# Pressing and Gripping with Screws

This is a wine press. You can see the big screw thread in the center.

Screw threads make forces larger and increase the effort we make to help fix objects tightly together. We can also use them to help squeeze and grip things.

## Pressing with Screws

Presses crush grapes or apples to squeeze all the juice out of them. The juices are then used to make wine, cider, or bottled fruit juices.

## How Presses Work

A press is made up of a large tub with a long screw thread in the center. On the thread is a nut, and attached to the nut is a long handle and a disk that fits neatly into the tub, like a **piston**. Winding the handle around moves the nut down, which pushes the disk down onto the fruit. The force on the fruit is much larger than the effort used to turn the nut.

Vices have screw threads for gripping benches, and threads for gripping objects.

## Holding Tight

A vice is a tool for holding objects firmly while they are being cut, shaped, or drilled. A vice has two sides, called jaws. One side is fixed, and one side slides backward and forward. The sliding jaw is moved by a screw thread. Turning the thread by its handle forces the jaws together, gripping things between them very tightly.

# A Screw Press

This experiment shows how a screw can be used as a simple machine to crush things. This kind of machine is called a screw press.

**1** Put one nut onto the bolt and turn it until it is halfway along the nut. Put a washer on the bolt and slide it down to the nut.

**2** Pierce a hole in the center of the cardboard. Slide the cardboard down the nut to the washer. Add the other washer and then the other nut.

**3** Turn the nuts in opposite directions with your fingers until the washers are tight against the cardboard. Now turn them as much as you can with the wrenches.

**4** Undo the nuts again. Take out the cardboard to see how it was squashed.

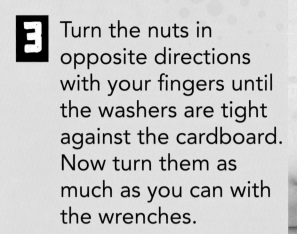

## So Simple!

Turning the nuts made them move toward each other, squashing the cardboard. The wrenches let you turn the nuts with a large effort. The screw threads on the bolts made this force much bigger, so the washers squeezed the cardboard.

# Screws in the Past

Nobody knows who invented the screw, but there is plenty of evidence that screws were in use around 2,500 years ago. In ancient Rome, people were using screws for some of the jobs they use them for today. These include crushing grapes and olives and pressing clothes to squeeze water from them.

## An Ancient Water Pump

The Archimedean screw is a type of water pump. It is made up of a wide pipe with a screw thread fitted tightly through the center. When the lower end is put into water and the screw is turned, the screw scoops up water and carries it to the upper end. The Archimedean screw is named after the famous Greek mathematician Archimedes, but it was probably invented before he lived. The ancient Greeks used the screw to drain land and get water out of ship **bilges**. Archimedean screws are still used in some parts of the world.

*As an Archimedean screw turns, water is trapped and carried upward in its thread.*

## Printing By Pressing

In the 1430s, the German printer Johannes Gutenberg used a screw press to press paper onto **metal type** covered with ink to print books. Gutenberg built the first printing press, with a large wooden screw to force the paper downward. Gutenberg's press made it much quicker to print books than was possible before.

*The large wooden screw on this old printing press forces the paper downward.*

# Lifting and Adjusting with Screws

When you turn a nut on a bolt that is fixed in place, the nut moves along. Yet, when you turn a bolt that is through a fixed nut, the bolt moves along. People use these movements to lift objects and adjust their position.

## Lifting with Jacks

A screw thread turns the effort you make into a larger force, so you can use a screw thread to overcome the weight of a heavy object. All cars have a screw jack. The jack is used to lift up the car when a tire needs changing. A gentle push on the jack's handle turns a rod with a screw thread, and this overcomes the weight of the car, which is the load.

*This is a scissors jack. The screw thread pulls the two sides together.*

22

## Making Things Level

   Screw threads can be used to change the position of things. Heavy appliances, such as stoves and refrigerators, have feet mounted on screw threads, which allow you to make them perfectly level. Turning a knob on a foot moves the foot up and down. As the screw thread increases the effort you make, you can easily raise a corner of the appliance by turning its foot. **Tripods** for telescopes and cameras also have feet on screw threads so they can be made level.

*A camera mounted on a tripod makes it easier to take photographs on an uneven surface.*

# Moving with screws

Screw threads are useful for moving loose materials and liquids from place to place. As you turn a screw thread, the thread appears to move along. This effect is used to push material along. You have already seen one example of this—the Archimedean screw on page 20, which is used to raise water.

## Screw Transporters

A screw transporter is a machine that moves loose material around in a machine or a factory. A screw transporter has a screw thread with narrow shaft and a wide thread, inside a tube. When the thread turns, the vanes on the thread push the material along the bottom of the tube, from one end to the other. An example of this can be seen on a combine harvester, in which a screw transporter moves crops into the machine after they are cut down.

The screw transporter on a combine harvester has a right-handed screw and a left-handed screw.

A soil auger is a huge screw thread that digs holes for building foundations.

## Drilling

Screw threads are used in drilling. The part of a drill that does the cutting is called a drill bit. Sharp blades at the tip of the bit cut away material from the bottom of the hole being drilled. Behind the tip is a screw thread. As the drill bit spins, the thread pushes waste material backward and out of the hole.

# Lifting with screws

A screw jack is used to lift heavy objects, such as cars, by pushing them upward with a screw. Try this experiment to find out how they work.

## You Will Need:

- Tape
- A popsicle stick
- A nut to fit a bolt ¾ inch (18 mm) in diameter
- A bolt ¾ inch (18 mm) in diameter
- Thick cardboard
- A pair of scissors
- A ruler
- A pencil
- A washer to fit the bolt
- A small plastic pot
- A toy car

**1** Tape the popsicle stick to one side of the nut. Cut a piece of cardboard around 4 inches (10 cm) square. Tape the head of the bolt to the cut piece of cardboard.

**2** Wind the nut onto the bolt until it is around 2 inches (5 cm) down the bolt. Put the washer on the bolt so that it rests on the nut. Cut a piece of cardboard around 3 inches (8 cm) square. Pierce a hole in the center of this cardboard and fit it over the bolt, so that it rests on the washer.

**3** Put the plastic pot upside down on the cardboard. Put the toy car, on top of the pot. Turn the nut using the popsicle stick and watch to see what happens.

So Simple!

This simple screw jack shows how heavy objects can be lifted by hand using a screw as a simple machine. A light push on the handle pushed up the heavy car.

# Amazing Machines

Screws are simple, but handy, machines. They make our lives easier by increasing the effort we make. We use wood screws, fixing screws, and nuts and bolts mostly to fix objects tightly together. Screws also help us to grip objects, move materials around, and lift up heavy loads.

## What Did You Learn?

Have you tried the simple experiments in the book? What did you learn about screws?

## In Big Machines

Screws are simple machines that work on their own. However, we also find them in more complicated machines. Most machines have parts that are joined together with screws and nuts and bolts. Turning screw threads often moves the parts of a machine up or down, or backward or forward.

*This screw thread is called a worm gear. When it turns, it turns the gear.*

## Can't Live Without Them

Humans have been using screw threads for thousands of years. Screws might be simple, but it would be impossible for us to live without them. There are probably more of them around than you think! Most of the appliances and gadgets we use every day, and many of the fixtures and fittings in our homes, have screws in them. Keep an eye out for screws wherever you go!

*Small nuts and bolts join up the parts of this toy car.*

# Glossary

**bilges** (BIL-jez)  Spaces in the bottom of ships' hulls.

**bradawl** (BRAD-ol)  A tool with a tough metal spike, ised to make small holes in wood before putting in a screw.

**forces** (FORS-ez)  Pushes or pulls.

**hexagonal** (heks-A-guh-nul)  Having six equal sides.

**inclined planes** (in-KLYND-PLAYNS)  Slopes used as simple machines.

**levers** (LEH-vurs)  Rods or bars used as a simple machines.

**load** (LOHD)  The push or pull that a screw overcomes, which may be the weight of an object.

**magnitude** (MAG-nih-tood)  The measurement of something's strength.

**metal type** (Meh-tul TYP)  Small blocks of metal with raised letters at one end.

**piston** (PIS-ton)  A tube with a disk or short cylinder that moves up and down against a liquid or gas, to move something.

**pulleys** (PU-leez)  Wheels with ropes around them that work as simple machines.

**screws** (SKROOZ)  Simple machines with inclined planes wrapped around cylinders.

**screw thread** (SKROO THRED)  The spiral groove around a screw or bolt.

**tripods** (TRY-podz)  Supports or stands with three legs.

**wedges** (WEJ-ez)  Triangular objects used as simple machines.

**weight** (WAYT)  The force of gravity on an object, which pulls the object downward.

**wheel and axles** (WEEL AND AK-sulz)  Simple machine made up of disks with fixed bars running through their centers.

# Read More

To learn more about screws, check out these interesting books:

Challen, Paul. *Get to Know Screws*. Get to Know Simple Machines. New York: Crabtree Publishing Company, 2009.

Dahl, Michael. *Twist, Dig, and Drill: A Book About Screws*. Amazing Science: Simple Machines. Mankato, MN: Picture Windows Books, 2006.

De Medeiros, Michael. *Screws*. Science Matters: Simple Machines. New York: Weigl Publishers, 2009.

Gosman, Gillian. *Screws in Action*. Simple Machines at Work. New York: PowerKids Press, 2010.

Walker, Sally M., and Roseann Feldman. *Put Screws to the Test*. Searchlight Books: How Do Simple Machines Work? Minneapolis, MN: Lerner Publications, 2012.

# Websites

For web resources related to the subject of this book, go to: www.windmillbooks.com/weblinks and select this book's title.

# Index